Why Storms
are Named After People
and Bullets
Remain Nameless

Tanaya Winder

For any heart that has survived a storm or bullet
may you mosaic back together the pieces
& embrace the healing that was (and is) always yours.

Contents

Dear Heart,   6

We Are Made of Stars   8

Every Word You Ever Needed   9

I'll Be Seeing You   10

What It Takes To Disappear   13

Pay Attention to What You Feed   14

like any good indian woman   15

We Were Stolen   17

Surviving the Elements   18

Chasing Storms   20

For Girls and Women on Fire   21

resistance   22

Why Storms are Named After People
    & Bullets Remain Nameless   25

Thirteen Ways of Loving a Blackbird   28

This Unfolding   33

The Healing   34

Constellations of Love   35

Hearts on Fire   37

Each Year I Travel Through   38

Dear Heart,

I am ready to tell you about the reckoning,
the lessons of surviving a bullet or storm.

I want to teach you how to breathe again,
so you can understand how a heart learns

to beat again. to beat again. to beat
again. breathe again.

How do traumas eat dinner at the same table?

And do they pray together, before or after eating?

*

Is it possible to love the gun that shot you?

Or will you always blame the bullet?

And Bullets Remain Nameless

We Are Made of Stars

we are made of stars
we know who we are
we know where we've been
& what we survived
all our ancestors did to keep us alive
it's inside you, their light guides you

we are made of stars
we know who we are
together as constellations
we carry generations
in each beat of our hearts
it's what sets us apart.

we are made of stars.

Every Word You Ever Needed

I am a woman who can grow in the dark
with a glow-in-the-dark heart.

The moonlight is calling me softly:
have the courage to be brave and create,

now's the time. Write
every word you ever needed.

I'll Be Seeing You

*Suicide is the 2nd leading cause of death for AI/AN youth
ages 15-24*

Some days I exist in a parallel plane,
spend my nights in another universe
where you are with me, or at least very near.
We go to that same secret spot in the corner of the park.
bring martinelli's sparkling cider and pretend
we're toasting to us – This. Days like this we seem star far
from our shadows, the darkness no longer attached to us,

Our hearts try to breathe light
like we both already know you're the question
I'll spend every poem trying to answer.
So I sing a song to remind us of the moon

*"I'll be seeing you in all the old familiar places
That this heart of mine embraces all day through
In that small café, the park across the way,
The chestnut tree, the wishing well"* *

Where I wish you well I wish you well I wish….
I could have loved the black hole right out of you
that night. In another universe my voice is echoing
come back to me, come back to me, come back
It's the Halloween you runaway.
Dressed as a referee blowing whistles
and that night I was the Devil. You danced with me
while we swayed like branches bent
with the burden they were born to carry.

Why Storms are Named After People

I wish I could stop writing this poem
that I could get over longing to travel back in time to find us
daydreaming into sleep wondering what it feels like
to carry such sweetness in holding another life.

Somewhere along the way beautiful fruit is falling
they've been tricked into thinking they're rotting
And I want to sing them into holding on a little longer.
Because now I know –

in another universe one of us is the branch,
the other the fruit.
But we can't tell who is who
or when to let go.

*lyrics from Billie Holiday's "I'll Be Seeing You."

And Bullets Remain Nameless

How do wounds make love?

*

If you've spent decades drowning in dry heaving sorrow,

Can you still remember what it feels like to breathe?

*

Can ghosts forgive if you've stopped grieving them?

Why Storms are Named After People

What It Takes To Disappear

Tell me again that my kisses are magic
that my mouth unfolds longing like a landslide.
Loneliness spills over my lips each time you ask:
sing for me. Your unquenchable thirst devours

each syllable. Tell me again how you wanted to paint
the way you see me because I know all the words
to the first song you made love to in the back seat
of a red car, windows down overlooking the desert at sunset.

Tell me you didn't forget to pay those parking tickets,
and to take your paintbrush out of the water, or
the way we fit together like puzzle pieces and
that once we slow danced, cheek-to-cheek

in the middle of the street, then hop-scotched
on the dotted lines all the way back to our childhoods
playing hide-and-seek. You told me once you didn't
want to be left behind. Now you're always leaving

the door wide open. I want to nail shut all possibilities
because the sun is already setting. The sky is red and
we're driving the car on a road to nowhere through the desert.
The sand is so hot it burns. Tell me you'll quit hiding, and seek.

See, the car is already melting, you left your paintbrush
in the water, and we're dissolving into red, the oils of our skin,
Our memories blur. How do you see me?
You painted a desert, red and the car

falling apart. Tell me we dreamt it all and
when I open my eyes to see: I won't remember. You,
tell me the next time I open my mouth to sing
the magic of it all will make me disappear.

Pay Attention to What You Feed

Sometimes it's those you love
& those who love you who eat the most hungrily,

& finding the strength
to love yourself becomes your toughest work.

like any good indian woman

i pull my brothers from words, *stupid injun,* shot like bullets. when people ask why my brothers hated school i say: the spirit remembers what it's like to be left behind when america took children from homes, displaced families with rupture, ripping a child's hand from a mother's to put them in boarding school buildings. my brothers are mourning a loss they try to fix in finding home in another person, so they travel from reservation to city singing blues and 49 songs about love.

       i pull my brothers from cars named after indians: *navajo, cherokee, & tacoma.* on a danger destined road my brothers are born longing for a way back from relocation & long walks across miles & miles & miles of removal. my brothers search for themselves in unhealthy addictions disguised as makeshift bandages.

       i pull my brothers from bottles they think answers might be hidden at the bottom of. my brothers stumble through back alleys looking for a love & laughter that was stolen from them like the land. and when their brown bodies try to find healing & love, other brown bodies cringe at their touch because like any good indian woman, our bodies are connected to an earth, still being raped by the pipelines forcibly laid down inside all that we hold sacred. and my brothers hold onto their colonial emotional baggage so tightly they think its gravity

       so i pull my brothers from oceans believing they deserve the hurt so much they nearly drown themselves in it. and sometimes my brothers knife ancestral grieving onto their wrists, slits to remember the only time we are ever red, skinned is when blood flows from the open wounds america knifed onto our brown skin. self-love: apply pressure.

i pull my brothers from ashes.
america tried to burn us not knowing we were already flame.

& these will be the stories i tell my grandchildren when one day,
they ask me – why being a good indian woman means we burn
like phoenix repeatedly pulling our brothers.

Why Storms are Named After People

We Were Stolen

One day when we're all gone
    and you think we've disappeared.

You'll realize we were stolen. The earth
    will continue to split herself open in mourning.

    The morning sun will no longer rise because you failed
to protect those who are so powerful they're in sync with the moon.

    And soon, hurricane, tsunami high waves will cover the land
in the water you didn't care to protect because

you thought oil was more precious than life.
    Our Mother will shake in her wailed grieving so hard

to stir you from complacency. Pipelines will break
    and the fractured sites will turn flame

    as Mother Earth sets herself on fire.
And as you're being swallowed whole

    you'll wish you paid more attention, wish you listened,
wish you believed, wish you protected

instead of abused or misused us.
    Don't just bear witness at rallies or see us in headlines

that declare "missing" then "body found" then "murdered"
    and then claim that you'll protect us.

    See us when we're alive
not just when we go missing, get stolen, and murdered.

    Remember that we are real, we are worthy, and
we deserve to be seen with each beat our hearts take,

    each beat our hearts make
as we continue to birth revolutions.

And Bullets Remain Nameless

Surviving the Elements

Some lessons come softly,
others burn like wild fire
     & these are often the most important lessons

because they come so intensely & quickly,
but they always present you with a choice:
     become engulfed by the flames and burn, then wait
        to rise

born anew from the ashes –
or, transform into flame,
     becoming the fire itself. You can choose

to be a fire burning brightly,
igniting healing & passion into other hearts
     because you survived the very elements that tried to
        defeat you.

Why Storms are Named After People

Can you love the storm that ruined you?

*

Can a bullet make its way back into a gun?

*

What started all of this blooming?

And Bullets Remain Nameless

Chasing Storms

I heard once, a rupture chooses who it wants to break
the way a barrel chooses the bullet.
I walked away from (what I thought was) love
listening to the sounds of thunder.
He kissed me like lightning but he fell apart like rain

The first man I loved painted his organs outside of his body,
brush stroked his heart into beating again and again
He held whole notes in his hands, and a marching band inside
    his heart.
And he played song after song to keep us from falling apart
We were chasing storms, but forgot about the lightning.

He kept asking if I knew about surrender.
If surviving meant exploding like thunder
As we chased away the grey, whispering wishes like prayers
I should have seen what was going to happen next.
He parted his lips then slowly pulled out petal after petal of red
until his mouth flowered a wilted bouquet of questions.

How do wounds make love?
When you're struggling with whether or not you're enough
can we stitch back together our broken
With all these words left unspoken?

Why Storms are Named After People

For Girls and Women on Fire

Everything happens for a reason
and breaks you thought were heartaches was really Creator
helping you dodge a massive bullet destined for danger,
    rupture,
and the darkness you crawled your way out of long ago.

So let go.

Let go of anything that didn't work out the way you wanted.
Because you know this, deep in your heart of hearts, you know:
you were born from a line of fierce women on fire,
who shine light in the darkest of places, and heal those in need.

And if people are afraid of you
(let them be afraid)
they should be.

Because you are powerful beyond containment;
the kind of free people dream of embodying
and everything is coming together the way it was always
    destined.

Because you are destined for greatness
and anything you ever set your mind to,
you looked yourself in the mirror and said
"We are going to do this."

And you did.

You did do it. So don't stop now.
Because you are meant to
keep all of the promises you ever made to yourself.

And Bullets Remain Nameless

resistance

noun re•sis•tance \ri-ˈzis-t'n(t)s\
1: to exert oneself so as to counteract or defeat
2: to withstand the force or effect of

Oh Say can you see, by the dawn's early light
what so proudly we hailed at the twilight's last gleaming
whose broad stripes and bright stars through the perilous fight
o'er the ramparts we watched were so gallantly streaming…*

and the concussion grenade's red glare, water cannons bursting
   in freezing air
temperatures, and rubber bullets shot at water protectors gave
   proof
through the night that Amerikkka is still spelled with 3 K's
America, a word that starts with an A turned upright like
   pointed white hood,
saluting the settler colonialism, ism, ism – a dangerous
   definition, or Doctrine
of Discovery buried in the highest Court of the land, Supreme.
Supremacy of the free, home of the brave braves, who became
   animals upon "discovery"?
But you can't discover a people who already existed,
And you cannot find something that was never lost.
Even an Indigenous holocaust couldn't get us written about in
   history books.
Our numbers may not be written on arms, but you can count
   the amount of headstones
from children buried in Indian Boarding Schools.
America, thought we died there when they cut our hair,
   stabbed our tongues into silence,
Pried our mouths open into singing anthems of freedom in
   English. A language

Why Storms are Named After People

America force-fed down our throats, like a pill called
    assimilation telling us to let go
of all we hold sacred like our connection to the land, by
    moving us onto reservation
into desolation, a symbolic annihilation so deafening today
    people forget we exist
or that we are real, never seeing beyond the painted faces of
    Washington. Redskins.
This corporate colored Red, skins our identity and bleeds
in a country built on the backs of brown bodies,
genocide and slavery. what do those stars & stripes represent
when those in power won't honor our treaty rights.
Who's right? When we all have a right to survive and be free –
to live, to drink clean water, and not build walls around these
    manmade borders.
When history is written by colonizers they are always heroes.
Colonizer made from colon, body politic, a black snake
    swallowing everything.
a black snake swallowing everything. a black snake swallowing
    everything.
when they're drilling in the name of money, and killing our
    water & soil in the name of oil
and our sisters are being stolen, and the holes we dig in the
    earth mirror
the holes we keep digging in ourselves, we keep digging in
    ourselves
And who can tell what the real truth is when alternative facts
    are birthed in
a colonial womb. But the revolution will never be won through
    patriarchy,
or held in the fists or lips of patriarchal men. But it will be
    born from women
who know how to carry movements in the womb of
    intertwining lives,

And Bullets Remain Nameless

The revolution will be birthed from women who know that
    deliverance and delivery
come from being ripped open in an unstoppable force that
    reminds us:
our most powerful weapons will always be giving life,
and a body in prayer that stands up unafraid to speak
Can you see me? Can you see us when you sing....?
Oh Say does that star spangled banner yet wave O'er the land of
    *the free**
"and the home of the brave"
you have the right to remain silent
but you also have the right not to be.

*lyrics from "The Star-Spangled Banner"

Why Storms are Named After People

Why Storms are Named After People & Bullets Remain Nameless

"I reach out in love, my hands are guns, my good intentions are completely lethal." – Margaret Atwood

My body is a canvas. He painted
my eyes as hurricanes swelling with questions. I never ask –
which brush is your favorite? Or,

one day *when you paint my heart
outside of my body will you use all of your favorite colors?* Only
    the best ones
cover up a vessel's holes,

storm torn linen stretched too thin.
Modern-day marksman, Orion-the-hunter, finger on trigger.
My eyes hold his in orbit:

Look at *me*, too afraid. He will get lost there.
So I pluck my eyes from skull. *Teach me how to breathe the colors
I could never see without you.*

Unintended impact. His stray-bullet-heart
ricocheted into mine like a painting we didn't mean to step into
with Sagittarius pulling back

bow to enough tension to hold
this milky way's center. Take aim, fire – an arrow across a universe
where we spiral together through

the time we wish we had
more (or less) of. There, we'll rediscover open wounds. Longing
for closure, his mouth opens –

I like the way you fit inside me,
without want. But, I wanted us to fall without loss, domino-effect,
arms outstretched, trust

fall, open, graceful. In another life
we drank in all of the constellations, tasted each star, then
    committed
light to memory

so we could always navigate our way
back to each other. He will leave me on a starless night. When
    I wake
I'll find my eyes inside an ashtray

burning, beside his
goodbye note: *Tell me you'll never forget this. Your love is a universe*
too big, too innocent.

Before the sun rises, I'll place my eyes back,
inside out. I want to see everything I was ever afraid of. I want
to know what to (if I should) name him.

Why Storms are Named After People

Where does fear live inside your body?

       And how, do you house it there?

      *

Can the mouth call back love if it didn't last?

      *

Can the tongue change love to enough before it touches teeth?

And Bullets Remain Nameless

Thirteen Ways of Loving a Blackbird

I.
First, notice the way she flies –
her wings spread wider than fear could ever reach.

II.
Pay attention to her darkness
as the blackbird dives
then rises
towards the sun.

This flight
is how she heals
hearts.

III.
Consider the blackbird's grace.
Imagine the balance it takes her
to carry such weight while holding light.

IV.
Be careful
of becoming too hungry
for the blackbird's call.

She is not a bridge to your ocean-wide wounds.

V.
Do not confuse her falling with flying.
Either way she doesn't need you to catch her.

Why Storms are Named After People

VI.
You and blackbird. Blackbird &
you – painted a bow, then
shot an arrow with a wish
to be loved, to be loved,
to be loved
into the multiverse
& blackbird fell
from the sky.

VII.
(Never fall for someone
meant to fly.)

You'll fall for blackbird.
She'll ask you,
"What would you say
to the next person who loves me?"
You'll say, *"I'd tell them not to cage you."*

VIII.
When you tell blackbird
you love her, but leave anyway
she'll think of all the words she doesn't have yet.

IX.
Blackbird still carries the arrow.

X.
Blackbird won't realize it in the beginning,
But you'll have set her free.
She'll find herself in tracing
the outlines of her wings.

XI.
The blackbird rises
from the ashes of breaking.

And Bullets Remain Nameless

XII.
Whenever someone opens their mouth
to say the word *love*
a blackbird releases
into the sky of another universe.

XIII.
Open your eyes,
now watch blackbird fly.

A Song for Redemption

My mouth is a cave, calloused with housing your name.
The overgrowth molds the air. I inhale
our memories slowly in
and out through lips parted

open. This is how we lived –
breaking like orange peel skin, edges inexact
and me trying to stitch jagged scraps.
Who was the last
to suckle sweetness, mouth around flesh?
The juice of everything I never told you
inching down my chin.

Imagine this overflowing:
light exploding as a thousand stars
sentenced themselves to the ocean. After you
died, I drank in waves –
tried flooding my veins to change
my inner landscape. Guilt.
I drowned, swallowed mouthfuls,
until I became drunk on ghosts.

Your name haunts the tip of my tongue.
A survivor's guilt lump takes root in
my throat's stem, threatening to explode
the cold I've learned to live with.

My heart named itself a stray
    bullet, intent on rediscovering all the holes
        no song was big enough to stop the bleeding –
      heart, yours a black hole
    I spent nights trying to love out of you.
   My fingers couldn't grasp its edges
so I used my voice to unzip each scar

to climb inside your fear. I found us there
    continuously swimming from shore through sea
        just to be caught two-stepping on the fiery
      ship's deck
        while the radio plays our favorite song,
      the one with the voice grainy –
   breadcrumbs we can trace our way back
through any river, city, landscape, or

ruin. I can still taste the sound
   in the search for redemption
      (mouth full of ash) now I know
        what it's like to burn beautifully.

Why Storms are Named After People

This Unfolding

What holds us together after an explosion or storm?
This heart unfolding and un-
                              folding into one

thousand paper cranes, *No, blackbird.*
Remember you are a blackbird
                              rising from the ashes of

every fire that tried to burn you into nameless.
Close your eyes. Make a wish.
                              Open your mouth. Name it.

The Healing

By the time you hear this you might think it's too late,
it's your fate to give up to give in never win.
If you feel lost in an uphill battle inside your heart,
It's the hunger that's tearing you apart.

But, you need to feed your spirit, let it breathe.
Grieve the ghosts that show you where scars bleed
Follow the ache to see where it all starts—
choosing to heal is the hardest part.

Constellations of Love

& when i remembered i was magic, it unraveled into
  beautiful moonlight
exposing new stars to wish upon.

& then something wonderful happened.

& the wonder that happened became constellations
of all the love i ever dreamt of.

& all the promises i ever made myself started coming true

& my heart expanded to carry more than i thought possible
like the ocean holding a sky full of stars full of light

full of fire bursting the kind of love
light that radiates the energy that holds us together.

What does unfolding feel like?

*

Can I call my spirit back if I say my name four times?

*

Can the heart mosaic itself back together after it has been broken?

*

Is it possible to spread your wings wider than fear or doubt could
ever reach?

Why Storms are Named After People

Hearts on Fire

We each carry a fire in our hearts
an undying flame burning so brightly
it can barely be contained
in these earthbound bodies. This fire
can never be extinguished –
our ancestor's sang songs that sparked its breathing.
The fire we carry gives us meaning and purpose.
Some call it life, call it passion,
call it gift. Call it spirit –
name it *magic*, for it has always been
y(ours), fully. We move through the world together,
interconnected with w(hole) heart, scars & all.
Because you are everything
that ever happened to you.
You. Are. Here. You are love(d)
Remember you are fire.
And you cannot make fire feel afraid,
so be brave in the healing of yourself & others.
Be a warrior of revolutionary, legendary love.

Each Year I Travel Through

Year One.

I pass the line of semis carrying a bridge just before entering a city named Echo.

I wish I knew what it meant to connect and be connected.

So I roll down all the windows and whisper into the wind – *what are you so afraid of?*

Year Two.

I keep hoping one day I'll hear my voice travel back to me.

Instead, I teach my students how to hold words in pieces: sound, history, impact, and beginnings.

Take for instance *colonized.* Etymology. Colon: body politik. Imagine it inside your body, a snake swallowing everything.

Year Three.

Someone who once took my love wrote to me: *Love is a verb. Our existence is verbing.*

I said *took* but I should really say *stole.*

Year Four.

I have been undoing ever since. Trying to write my way back to a beginning. So I recall an end. The memory of the year when he told me he wanted to travel backwards like an echo finding its way back to a throat's cavern.

Why Storms are Named After People

I can't remember the exact words he used when he left me but flies circled our table like vultures. They sounded what I was too afraid to admit.

This love was rotting.

Year Five.

The stench swallowed everything.

Year Six.

Remember: from Latin *rememorari*, meaning *"recall to mind"*

The 1ˢᵗ time I taught poetry the students kicked a blackbird outside on the grass. I saw them through the window and ran out to stop them. It was already dead but I asked anyway: *why would you do that?*

They said, *pain demands to be felt.*

Year Seven.

Pain was holding myself in pieces:

> Black feathers on the ground like petals
> plucked from their center pulled off one by one,
> year by year. Post-wish dandelion seeds scattered
> into the wind like parachutes awaiting
> the impact of falling.

Year Eight.

Healing was pain, asking: *Can you feel me?*

Year Nine.

Name it.
Then choose to let go.   Let go.   Let go.

Year Ten.

If I close my eyes I can see a window. On the other side I am a child playing, happy, laughing, and free. I feel the magic and light I was before pieces of me were stolen, then carried away.

I see me.

I am swinging, kicking my legs up until my feet touch sky. I am imagining I am going to fly. Before I jump, I whisper to my child self: *It's okay. It's okay to fall. And when you get lost, remember —*

> *Love returns in pieces.*
>
> *Don't be afraid.*
>
> *One day, you'll find words*
>
> *for everything.*

Acknowledgements

Special Thanks to the author's portrait artist Karina McMillan.

Bio:

Karina McMillan is a Lumbee artist who lives in Red Springs, North Carolina. She has been drawing and painting even before she could even remember. She and her parents first realized her talent when she won the mascot drawing contest for her elementary school while she was in second grade. From that point, she completely immersed herself into art. Karina has gone on to enter her artwork into many contests that range from local, regional, state, and national. For the past 4 years she has entered her work into the Robeson County Fair, with one piece going to the North Carolina State Fair. Her success in this confirmed her dedication and love for creating art, which pushed her to enter her work into bigger contests. In May 2016, she won the Congressional Art Show for the 8th Congressional District of North Carolina. Her proudest achievement is when she won a Silver Medal in the National Scholastic Art and Writing Awards for her self portrait in April 2017. She currently attends Lumberton Senior High School in Lumberton, North Carolina, and she will be graduating in June 2017.

Artist Statement:

Being a self-taught artist has been an extremely rewarding experience. Over the years, my art has grown extraordinary. I enjoy sharing my art and want to use it to help start meaningful conversations about the importance of art to the world. I currently am skilled in graphite, charcoal, colored pencil, pen and ink, acrylic paint, and watercolor. I strive for my pieces to look as lifelike as possible by capturing the beauty that the model holds. My art teacher, Scotty Thompson, has continually pushed me to be the best artist that I am able to be. I will be attending the University of North Carolina at Charlotte beginning in the Fall of 2017, and I will be majoring in Fine Arts with a concentration in Illustration.

Instagram: **@karinas.art**
Facebook: **Karina McMillan's Art**
YouTube: **Karina McMillan**
Website: **https://karinamac98.wixsite.com/artportfolio**

Special Thanks to the cover artist Monique Bedard (Aura)

Bio:

Monique Bedard (Aura) is Haudenosaunee (Oneida) artist who grew up in Courtright, Ontario. She has been deeply and passionately involved in visual arts for more than a decade. She moved to Lethbridge, Alberta to complete a Bachelor of Fine Arts (Studio Art). In 2010, she returned to Ontario where she began instructing group art lessons with children, youth and adults. Monique currently resides in Tkaronto as an artist, muralist and workshop facilitator. She is a Diploma Toronto Art Therapy Candidate working on the completion of a major project titled "Our Stories Our Truths: an Art-Based Storytelling Project" with an emphasis on art as healing.

Artist Statement:

I am inspired by storytelling and the healing journey, individually and as a community. Currently, I combine painting, drawing, beadwork, image transfers, and collage to examine stories that are connected to the mind, body, and spirit. I aim to address the pain of intergenerational trauma and intergenerational healing to communicate experiences from the inside out. By unearthing my own stories, I am able to strengthen connections where the process creates awareness and understanding; this experience is ultimately part of the healing journey.

My newest series is titled, Akwelyá•ne | Kayá•tale' (My Heart | Portraits). There are so many times people in our communities are misrepresented or seen in a negative light. It is my goal with this series is to create portraits of people in a good way. Chief Lady Bird said that I put "emphasis on individual truths, reclamation of our identity, sovereignty over our bodies and emotions, and the importance of love," which is my intention. I also give people the option to share a story or quote that ultimately becomes the caption. Too often, other people decide what our stories are and I want my art to help people reclaim their stories.

Website: **auralast.wix.com/auralast**
Instagram: **@auralast**
Twitter: **@auralast**
Facebook: **aura.last.art**
Tumblr: **aurastuff.tumblr.com**

About the author

Tanaya Winder is a poet, vocalist, writer, educator, and motivational speaker from the Southern Ute, Duckwater Shoshone, and Pyramid Lake Paiute Nations. She received a BA in English from Stanford University and a MFA in creative writing from the University of New Mexico. Since then she has co-founded *As/Us: A Space for Writers of the World*, a literary magazine publishing works by Indigenous writers and people of color. A winner of the 2010 A Room Of Her Own Foundation's Orlando prize in poetry, her poems from her manuscript "Love in a Time of Blood Quantum" were produced and performed by the Poetic Theater Productions Presents Company in NYC. West End Press published her debut poetry collection *Words Like Love* in 2015. She is the Director of the University of Colorado at Boulder's Upward Bound program, which serves approximately 103 Native high school youth from across the country. She co-founded the *Sing Our Rivers Red* traveling earring exhibit to raise awareness about murdered and missing Indigenous women and girls. She is a 2016 National Center for American Indian Enterprise Development "40 Under 40" list of emerging American Indian leaders recipient and a 2017 First Peoples Fund Artists in Business Leadership fellows. Finally, she is the founder of Dream Warriors, an Indigenous artists management company where she manages artists Tall Paul, Mic Jordan, and Frank Waln. Learn more about her work from the following:

Instagram: **@tanayawinder**
Twitter: **@tanayawinder**
Facebook: **facebook.com/tanayajwinder/**
Website: **www.tanayawinder.com**

Made in the USA
Lexington, KY
17 October 2017